CW00687690

Gallery Books
Editor: Peter Fallon

O BRUADAIR

Michael Hartnett

O BRUADAIR

Selected poems of Dáibhí O Bruadair
translated and introduced by Michael Hartnett

Gallery Books

O Bruadair
was first published
simultaneously in paperback
and in a clothbound edition
on 4 December 1985.
Reprinted 2000.

The Gallery Press
Loughcrew
Oldcastle
County Meath
Ireland

ISBN 0 904011 90 9 (*paperback*)

The Gallery Press acknowledges the financial assistance
of An Chomhairle Ealaíon / The Arts Council, Ireland,
and the Arts Council of Northern Ireland.

Contents

for Desmond and Olda Fitzgerald

Introduction

It is not rare for a poet to be obsessed with the work and mind of
another poet. The obsession can express itself in many ways — scorn
(which is often public), awe before a massive superiority (which is
always private), and love (which can become a bore to readers who do
not share the obsession). I have been obsessed by the work and mind
of Dáibhí O Bruadair and, though I certainly loved them and him, my
obsession usually expressed itself in frustration. And it has done so
since 1954, when I was thirteen. Like many Irish children I was
reared on a diet of folktale, Republicanism and mediocre ballads. I
knew some Gaelic but it was merely another school subject, not a key
to another culture. But in 1954, a friend, Seán Brouder, told me of O
Bruadair. He recited some verses which he translated for me. He
claimed that the poet had been born in my own town (Newcastle
West, Co. Limerick) and had lived most of his life in my own county,
and further, that he was buried in Monagay churchyard, not far from
Newcastle West. I was enthralled. I knew what poets looked like from
their portraits in library books, so I invented my own picture of O
Bruadair. The following year I wrote and published my first poem —
in English.

A man in his sixties and a boy of thirteen discussing, in a decrepit
country town, the life and work of a poet who had been dead for over
two hundred and fifty years, a poet of an extinct society whose works
were not published in his lifetime and which were now available only
in distant city libraries: this event, I later saw, profoundly illustrated
the obstinacy of the Irish mind, its constant connection with the past.
Even though I did not read a word of O Bruadair's until the late
'fifties, he had become for me the symbol of what I wanted to be. But
when I read him, in some school anthology of Gaelic verse, I was

shocked. I could not understand him! It seemed a gnarled, concertina'd kind of Gaelic, written for a distant and savage people. I went for consolation to the more accessible fields of Hopkins, Yeats and Eliot. I continued to read simpler Gaelic poetry, most of it written in the two centuries before O Bruadair's death. Why was my hero so unapproachable? How could an old man quote him with so much reverence and fluency? I determined in 1962 not to let him escape me, to unravel his language and to restore him as my idol. I still have not done so to my satisfaction.

The name O Bruadair (Brouder, Broderick) has been found in West Limerick since the ninth century: it is possibly of Danish origin. The poet Dáibhí was born about 1623. As is the case with most Gaelic poets our information on him is scant, but a number of details can be gleaned from his poetry. One of my dreams vanished when I read that it was unlikely that he had been born in Newcastle West but more probably in the barony of Barrymore in East Cork. My addiction to his work, however, did not vanish, and at least I found that he had lived most of his life in County Limerick, where his main patrons were the Fitzgeralds of Springfield (Gort na Tiobraid), near Broadford, and the Burkes of Cahirmoyle. Patronage was still deemed essential to a poet's survival: there were no publishers, no royalties, no grants; there were gifts, hospitality, cattle, horses, clothing and, sometimes, gold. But the Gaelic poet was no mere pensioner. O Bruadair was a recorder of his race's history and because of his place of birth two great local Norman-Irish families, the Fitzgeralds and the Burkes, became the symbols of that race for him. Indeed he did not write for the contemporary Burkes and Fitzgeralds, but for all of them who had ever existed and who ever would exist.

Living as he did throughout almost all of Ireland's most tragic century, he was also deeply immersed in the affairs of his time. Frank O'Connor said: 'The poetry of . . . David O Bruadair and a hundred other peasant poets is that of the sleepwalker; their thought is so much of the old dead world that it is as though a veil had fallen between them and reality'[1] This is not entirely true: O Bruadair was no peasant, and if there was a harking-back in his poetry there was also a looking-forward: his overall attitude to history (and in Gaelic society history *was* poetry) was cyclical. In his lifetime, while an active poet, he witnessed in Ireland the Popish Plot, the coming of

Cromwell, the Battle of The Boyne, the Treaty of Limerick and its non-ratification, the dispersal of the Irish leaders and their armies, and the selling into slavery (mainly to the Barbados) of thousands of women and children: these were fatal blows to an already tottering structure. But O Bruadair was no mere chauvinist. As his first translator, John Mac Erlean, S.J. (1870-1950), points out when speaking of the long poem 'An Longbhriseadh' ('The Shipwreck'): 'he ascribes all the misfortunes of his native land to the dissensions that prevailed among the (Irish) leaders and the insubordination of the irregular troops.'[2] In that poem O Bruadair says (I translate literally): 'I do not wonder at the foreigners' success: their agreements and friendships are discreet and lasting — not like my people's: their so-called unity would fall apart if pulled by a hair'. O Bruadair also believed that the dishonouring and disregarding of old customs contributed to their downfall — see page 26 — which very accurately reflects the minds of Irish country people today who maintain that the summers are bad because there is no longer any 'respect' for the old ways!

After 1690 O Bruadair's life assumed a pattern that was to become sadly commonplace among poets in the next few years: the *file*, the professional poet, the dignified chronicler of his race, gave way to a ragged horny-handed itinerant, muttering under his breath. Although O Bruadair's predicament was not unique, he felt, like many poets of his time, that he was the sole survivor, the last receptacle of Gaelic culture, and that his death would be the end for all. He was right, in a way. His death, and the death of the culture he stood for, was not a total annihilation: the eighteenth century was perhaps the most active time ever known for the production of poetry: but it was the *people*, rather than the professional poets, who began to sing; the poetry came out of cabins rather than castles. O Bruadair would have hated it. He would have looked down his nose at the sometimes flaccid extravagances of the Munster poets of the 1740s. But there had been a change of priorities: their purpose was to save a language, not a culture. Culture, as O Bruadair understood it, was gone. The style of poetry had already changed in his time: he wrote no songs but the poets of the eighteenth century seemed to write little else.

O Bruadair died, with his culture, in 1698, as we know from a manuscript written by the scribe Eoghan O Caoimh in 1702: *Dáibhí O Bruadair d'éag a mí January A. Domini 1698, et aduairt Eogan 'as trua liom a éag gan amhras'*. (Dáibhí O Bruadair died in the month of January AD 1698, and Eoghan said 'I really grieve for his death'.) It was always customary for Irish poets to write laments for their fellows. O Bruadair was famous in his lifetime, but there is no lament in Gaelic extant that mentions his death: this fact reflects the breakdown, the chaos of the 1690s.

O Bruadair, who wrote for his race, had a fierce and deep contempt for the lower-class Irish, the peasants, the little shop-keepers, the 'hucksters'. But this attitude was common among the professional Gaelic poets and even persisted right up to the 1740s. When I came to discover him for myself this aristocratic *hauteur* was something I disliked. Almost all my illusions were vanishing — but I was making the mistake of judging him by mid-twentieth century liberal standards — I had to reconsider his real position within his *own* society. He was 'anti-Irish' though he wrote in Gaelic: he was anti-clerical, though he was a Catholic — witness his satire on two priests (see page 20). He upheld and was upheld by what was left of the aristocracy of his time. He lived in an Ireland where for centuries the Holy Trinity was not so much Father, Son and Holy Ghost as Prince, Prelate and Poet. The Prince, to O Bruadair, had to have an impecc-able pedigree, had to be a cultured man and a generous one: he was the living symbol of Ireland: he did not own the land, he was married to it (more than once in the poems Ireland is referred to as a widow and as a deserted wife) and we must remember, a wife in Gaelic society was not the chattel she was under English law. So, to the end of his life, when he seemed just a beggar among beggars, O Bruadair remained an unrepentant aristocrat. Almost all his insults were aimed at the *dubh-thuataigh* (the black boors), the peasant Irish who immediately took to learning English language and customs *béarla binn* (simpering English) and *códaibh galla-chléireach* (foreign manners). But peasants in all ages are flexible — they have to be. O Bruadair took their action as a personal insult to himself, which it was not, and as an insult to Ireland, which it was. His bitterness was deepened all the more by the reversal of situations: illiterate peasants, now begin-ning to prosper, were able to sneer at the destitute poet. *Daoiste dubh díobaighthe duairc gan dán* one of them called him: 'a dirty-faced dour dumb-bell'.

But the unpleasant side of the poet's personality was the least of my difficulties: I had to face his poetry. Many would say that I have created an unnecessary and insurmountable barrier between myself and O Bruadair in my insistence that a poet who is such a consummate craftsman should be translated with obsessive care, that his techniques should be brought across as faithfully as possible. 'Poetry is that which gets lost in translation' is a widely-held notion: I do not agree with it. A poet/translator, if he loves the original more than he loves himself, will get the poetry across: he may even get the whole poem across or, at second best, force his own version — within the strictures laid down by the original author — as close as possible to poetry.

In O Bruadair's verse the translator is faced with opaque compound words: they look Germanic in their length and seem uncrackable. But I did to his poems what should be done to all poems: I read them aloud and slowly began to understand them. He uses archaic words: his compounds, though often a strange juxtapositioning of simple words, were sometimes inventions of his own (I must add he coined no *new* single words, but his binding together of often disparate ones created images that are almost surreal). Also, O Bruadair had a medieval mind, despite his century. Would that mind or the poetry that mirrored the mind be acceptable to a twentieth-century reader? The Gaelic poets' love for the art of poetry, for politics, religion, history and, above all, genealogy — these are his themes. Was it possible to make him attractive to our society with its fashionable and everchanging ragbag of sex, psychology and philosophies? In 1647, O Bruadair wrote a lament for his patron, Sir Edmond Fitzgerald. It contains four hundred and twenty lines, written in different metres, and enshrines the whole of the poet's attitude towards his world. But is it a poem we would accept today, whether we are Irish or not? Is it a poem in the sense that, say, 'The Deserted Village' is? It has music, stanzas, alliteration, rhyme — all the recognisable paraphernalia. But it is not a 'poem' and I have not included it in this selection. It is a ritual lament, a cry, given by the voice of a land for a husband of that land: the very trees and rivers cry, and their crying has nothing to do with pathetic fallacy. It goes beyond medievalism, back to a Celtic system where the whole world was alive.

O Bruadair's metres also presented a problem. Gaelic metres and poem-structures are notoriously complicated. Gerald Murphy in his *Early Irish Metrics* mentions eighty-four 'professional' metres (and there were hundreds of variations capable of being played on the 'non-professional' metres). If the seventeenth century saw the end of Gaelic society, it also saw the end of the professional poets, and their poem-structures went with them. O Bruadair witnessed this, but he adopted the new metres like the master he was. These 'new' metres of course were not new: they were the metres used by the lower ranks of versifiers and for peasant songs. *Sráid éigse,* O Bruadair called their users — 'street poets'. The professional poets had always used what they called *Dán Díreach,* 'direct compositions'. I call them 'poem-structures' to emphasize their uniqueness. They were not accentual metres: they were syllabic and had a very complex sound structure based on strict rules; even the consonants had values relative to each other. The popular metre (*amhráin*) were looser: they were accentual and were not bound by the rules of consonant-relation, but nevertheless, they were and are very difficult to master. Even though O Bruadair despised the changing times, he did move with them, complicating further the translator's task.

Because I wanted to find a way to make his poetry acceptable to our tastes, and to employ as much of his technique as I could master, I also wanted to find a 'voice' for him: and this task was most important of all. It was as difficult as finding a 'voice' for Milton in Chinese. I did not wish to afflict the poet with *my* voice: to do that, too much of what survived in my versions would be distorted. I kept his West Limerick audience before my mind and tried to convey how he would have come across to a literate but not scholarly public. I kept to his metres but simplified his diction. This is not meant to be a work of scholarship, but an attempt to restore and popularise. Perhaps I was fortunate here because no one had attempted O Bruadair on a large scale (James Stephens did some remarkable versions in his *Reincarnations,* 1918) since his first translator, whose style of English is no longer current. This, I hope, kept me free of influences. For instance, another Gaelic poet, Aogán O Rathaille, has found a 'voice' in Frank O'Connor's translations. And O'Connor, though he did not translate all of O Rathaille, has so powerfully become the 'voice' of that poet for our generation that anyone else who attempted to translate those poems could not help but fall into his (O'Connor's) cadences. But sufficient unto the generation are the translators thereof. O'Connor's versions of O Rathaille must soon be superseded, as will my versions of O Bruadair. O Bruadair could be funny, obscene and anguished. He had immense dignity and immense bitterness. If he is anti-democratic it is because he confused survival with betrayal. He was concerned with culture.

He would not have liked our Ireland.

Michael Hartnett

1. *Kings, Lords and Commons*, 1959, Preface.
2. *The Poems of David O Bruadair*, Vol. 1, Irish Texts Society, 1910.

'Bereft of its great poets . . .'

Bereft of its great poets
our old world's in darkness.
The orphans of those masters
offer answers that lack sharpness.

Their books are sadly mildewed —
books that were not flippant —
their lore unjustly *passé*,
though lore of wisdom-drinkers.

I pity the man who must witness the fate of himself,
now that poets are gone, who valued both wisdom and verse:
while their sons retain not one jot of that lore in their heads
old volumes disintegrate, dusty and mouldy, on shelves.

'The news let loose . . .'

The news let loose on tearful Ireland
grates on my ears by its reciting:
my tortured heart is unrequited —
he's gone today, who was once beside me.

I wish that I had died before him,
before the stones had slanted over him:
his heart's pulse was my heart's beating —
my care, my cure, my herb of healing.

Death's the theme of all my writing
till I am stretched in earth beside him:
because he, athletic, slim and playful,
lies abandoned in a lonely graveyard.

The sun with grief was near-demented,
water and earth and air lamented,
world and wave and moon were weeping,
land and fish and bird were grieving.

He was my love: lovely to watch him —
the look of his eye, his hair, his forehead,
white hands, white limbs and whiter shoulders —
breast like froth of a strong-waved ocean.

Farewell, my Norman-Irish sapling,
cunning glensman, mountain falcon,
delightful otter, man of magic,
a lion in strength, a bear in action.

Clever craftsman, no chief bolder,
priests' supporter, loyal soldier,
man of vision, prince of giving,
poet, hunter, man of wisdom.

Precious pillar, friend of poets,
help of heroes, apple golden,
learning's mirror in assemblies,
bright-limbed man who courted women.

My friend beneath that tombstone lonesome
I am sad I cannot go there:
I am here and you're encoffined —
that is not our old condition.

Till we meet again together
on doom's day's crowded hillside,
take my blessing and God's blessing:
as you are now, so all men finish.

Until we meet again, myself and my companion,
I must stay behind here, tortured and abandoned.
You must lie beneath this earth, which I sadly stand on:
My blessing go to God with you, my shy companion.

'I call ye ruffians . . .'

I call ye ruffians . . .! Not to ye for succour
can we turn, I swear by law:
ye lie befuddled in sops and puddles
suffering, fasting, pissing in straw.

Ye pair who huddle in meanness doubled
I ask, though troubled by such speech:
could the holy chapter do nothing apter
but make priests of characters the likes of ye?

Ye barrel-begrudgers to poetry authors,
ye sleep unapparelled
so your pockets won't be pawed with:
though I have no wish to slight *noble* fathers —
they were shifty bishops who gave *ye* holy orders!

'A shrivelled-up skivvy . . .'

A shrivelled-up skivvy, snappy, nosy, dry,
refused when a craving for booze ate my insides:
may she starve and a ghost over seas with her fly,
that wizened old midget who wouldn't one jorum supply.

I'd teach her a lesson if I really did pay her back
and the decent house-owners would give me on credit a cask:
though the beer was beside her I just got a bitter attack —
may the King of Glory not let her too long at her task.

An over-done slut with no note in her throat,
she flung and two-fingered me out of the door:
as to where she came out of, I can say no more —
small harm if she pupped a cat to a ghost.

She's no woman at all, that club-footed bitch,
with the driest old face you could meet on a trip:
she talks apishly now and she always will
and like a fool in her gruel may she dribble her shit.

'Because of the distress . . .'

Because of the distress to this girl caused —
she deserved no blow from this bull-calf —
and as most of her line are underground,
this hairy object I'm glad I can trounce.

I order his cloak to be kneaded in shit
and the lobes of his ears to be neatly clipped:
let him be whacked with a shovel of dung
and let boots like brushes polish his bum.

Let him be chased to the top of the hill
where he struck the young girl who did nothing to him
and with a cow-spancel let his nuts be tied up
as tight as can be, that swarthy young pup.

Barry, in battle since no one is bolder
and since your word is law all over,
unless your kin are sheltered from insulters
it'll be a great reproach to you in Munster.

'Though I had no money . . .'

Though I had no money in my keeping,
a surly tradesman I flattered sweetly:
I will write down for my readers
how I relieved of linen a crafty weaver.

Here is the Flattery:
Your father's purse was always open —
now, understand what is being spoken:
feeding me is a load on the locals —
don't let them feel their task is hopeless.

As I have no flocks nor herds in clover
and as they who used give have long passed over,
even a farthing, till my cows come homewards,
I could not give for a shirt to be woven.

Not even a farthing, (as I told you),
I have now in hand nor locked in my storeroom
the pelf of this robber world to pore on,
who left poets nothing and gave wealth to morons.

Myself, look here, I'm also a weaver,
but can't earn enough to cover my feet with:
if there's call for my craft before I leave here
I'll meet my debt — and more than meet it.

'Pity the man who English lacks . . .'

Pity the man who English lacks
   now turncoat Ormonde's made a come-back.
As I have to live here, I now wish
   to swap my poems for squeaky English.

'How daft this mode . . .'

How daft this mode of most of the men of Éireann
fattened newly with bold ostentation —
though rapt they pore on the *mores* of Gallic agents
their cant's no more than a ghost of garbled aping.

'All the same, it would make you laugh . . .'

All the same, it would make you laugh —
instead of the dances and games of the past
not a tittle is raised abroad in this land —
we ourselves have buried the summer at last.

Once all the girls of our world did play
mustered in companies on May Day:
now their cacophony tears my brain
as I witness their cunning, pointless games.

Our priests are scarred with greed and pride,
and all our poets are cut down to size:
but worst of all, I realise
that no one poor is considered wise.

Blast you, world, you sneaky bitch,
may your guts and liver in agony split!
What's it to you if I become rich?
You don't care when your children slip.

The once-proud men of this land have swapped
giving for gaining, culture for crap:
no tunes on the pipes, no music on harps —
we *ourselves* have buried the summer at last.

'To see the art of poetry lost . . .'

To see the art of poetry lost
with those who honoured it with thought —
its true form lowered to a silly chant,
sought after by the dilettante.

Those who write the Gaelic tongue
just mumble — when they should stay dumb —
the flaw's admired, the lack of passion —
now that doggerel is in fashion.

If one now writes to the proper rule
in the way demanded by the schools,
then some smart-alec Paddy or such
will say that it is obscure as Dutch.

God of Heaven, preserve and keep
the one man who protects from need
the climbers who scale true poetry
and avoid the lovers of English and ease.

Ámen.

'Pity I'm not total-yokel . . .'

Pity I'm not total-yokel
   (bad enough being *mere* yokel),
having to live among the locals
   — and they're surly folk here.

It's a pity I can't stutter
   like the rest of you good people,
for that would suit you better,
   you thick misguided creatures.

If I met a man who'd swap me
   I'd give him my pleasantries
and with this priceless wrap he
   could shield himself from peasantries.

There's more respect for fine feathers
   than respect for any talent —
O if what I spent on art-endeavours
   I'd spent on the latest fashions!

Though the chat and antics of those happy cannisters
lacks all wit and harmony, newness and clarity,
instead of spending all, wrestling with calligraphy,
I'm sorry I didn't spend it on vulgarity!

'I really believed him the boss of the town . . .'

I really believed him the boss of a town
or a chief of the blood of the noblest reknown,
this awful, illiterate, ignorant clown
who came from Magillivulgarity down.

This thick was a culchie-king down in south Clare
where the people pressed drink on him and all were amazed
when I went to a party and sat near his chair —
to find out if his dad had blue blood in his veins.

I craned my ear towards him, nearly down to his foot,
expecting a voice of a civilized cut:
when he opened his mouth after stuffing his gut,
I knew he was just a pig-ignorant scut.

'A wound has poured me . . .'

A wound has poured me a bowl of sickness
and left me shaken, taking my vigour,
since the tactics of our active men are
now defeated and their deeds are censored.

To the men of Ireland I am reciting
this tale of gall with all pity inside me:
a shame that they, dispersed in destitution,
are degraded and slain and looted.

All the able and daring princes
of the race that sailed from Spanish inlets —
their growing heirs in a day were scythed down,
their name, their fame, their rents and titles.

Hundreds are now vowing they're English —
stating that they are related to the victors
(people who breached gaps in thriving places,
maintained Irish estates and guarded trade-routes).

Vain is the trait of this cunning mother,
tricky and vexing, perverse and stubborn —
she's forsaken her race, her fierce raider-children
who first put a ring on the tip of her finger.

She consented to them: her hand she promised
and her love, to them, above foreign commerce:
she promised her blossom, her kiss, her dependance
to a Gaelic king and to all his descendants.

To that whoring female no change was ugly:
not her fate as bed-mate to all new snugglers —
though gaily, safely, richly, smugly
she laid with her old loves beyond insulting.

No danger then of plague or killing,
no injury, punishment or ill-feeling,
she had flocks and cattle and harness and vittles
in the days of the chiefs who sucked her nipples.

Noble and bold were her leading guardians
who in their time denied no almsgiving:
her women were gentle and loved conversation,
were witty, reserved, elegant and gracious.

Free from fault, all subtle in knowledge
were her bishops, her princes and her prophets
whose open hands were prone to offer,
till the day they died, those noble bulwarks.

Her shores were filled with fish from the ocean,
her badgers packed fat in every ditch-slope:
her trees leaned down at the end of autumn
with the crush of the crops that harvest brought them.

Her fleet at sea under sail and creaking
kept a look-out for doers of evil:
her white dwellings held angels at evening
and her low hills were laid out like deer-parks.

There's pain — but where are the war-skilled dragons?
Are they afraid of their own shadows?
A long time they were like swamp-land quaking
and so left Ireland open for the taking.

Many of this tribe survive as outcasts,
as misery and sin increase about them,
no love, no religion, no obedience —
each from the other meanly sneaking.

A tale of heartbreak is told, my friends now —
your culture doomed and you bewildered:
it will live until the earth has ending,
told by the old talking to their children.

'To them the state . . .'

To them the state has doled out nothing —
not a foot of land or a scrap of clothing:
but it will grant them a graceful favour —
let them safe to Spain by proclamations!

And then will come the fat-arsed slaggers
after trampling our culture and our manors,
pewtered, plated, brassy, baggaged,
the crop-head English with their pleasant accents.

All their hags will have beaver-fur mantles
and a dress of silk from head to ankles:
our castles will pass to upstart foragers —
old hands at swallowing cheese and porridge.

This is the gang, though I hate to name them,
who will live in bright motte and bailey:
Goody Hook and Mother Hammer,
Robin Saul and Father Psalm —
selling salt and wearing britches:
Gammer Ruth and Goodman Cabbage,
Mistress Capon, Kate and Anna,
Russell Rake and Master Gaffer!

Where once lived Déirdre the bright-born daughter,
long-haired Eimhear and the Grey of Macha,
where Aoibheall lived in her rocky mansion,
and the elegant ladies of Dé Danann,

there were schools of poets and story-tellers,
intricate dances, gastronomic pleasures,
arm-wrestling and restless soldiers waiting
to pierce with spears the target's framework.

O the going of those soldiers into graveyards
has split the hills of this old nation:
there is no music now but millstones grinding
and fog on the churches of this wife crying.

Humble loving Lamb, who had to carry
that black burden on your back to Calvary,
swiftly send us your help and blessing
and turn to us your bright face henceforth.

O Secret Love, no longer scold it,
the pride of these exhausted soldiers:
give back again the spark of courage
so they can repay their enemies' insults.

Obey the Lord who purchased sorely
peace for you, a heavenly omen:
come with spears and eager standard-bearers
and drive to doom these new-come aliens!

The Shipwreck

If I dare it, I swear on the Bible, and fear
the lines on my mind'll make a bitter song to hear
for the erring herd who turned a deaf ear
to the advice they received when freedom was near.

No cause for wonder how the newcomers get on —
they're careful in their councils, their friendships last long —
most unlike the woman's tribe to which I belong —
one pull of a hair and their closeness comes undone.

No wonder that our land, tangled in webs of sin
fell into misery through the crimes of her men —
for I know that her soldiers, under hardship's sting,
with malice and ignorance, set out pillaging.

Although I wrote an impartial document
of the fight and the might the Irish nobles spent
it would still be no sin to say in a song
that the bargain they made was no cowardly one.

And this is not the cant of flatterer or fools
who now dip their tongues to lick our leaders' boots:
to win any concession was a special marvel
against those English and mercenary arms!

Though our fierce raiding leaders were put behind bars
and their deaths threatened with every turn of war —
by their cleverness and mettle and their energy
many a soul from overthrowal they set free.

All those who couldn't stomach the just Articles
that were decreed for their relief by the king's will
their dog-in-the-manger attitude they'd soon yield
if they saw, as I saw, the homeless in the fields,

and children and women, sorry refugees
from Limerick to Kerry crying out in fear,
with nothing between them and the red sword's speed
but the might of their Christ and the eyes of their chiefs.

The decent race who kept the faith in the old cause
and held out in spite of fighting under unsure laws —
I cannot see, as factions see, their sailing off was wrong
though offered bribes to still reside where they belonged.

Each moderate man who thinks that he can live in peace
under the spears of the new chiefs who won the field
if his heart is pure and all are sure he has no blame,
no shame in it now to submit to the new reign.

The crowd that were roused (and I have heard of some)
to fight and kill upon the hills at the beat of the drum —
when, in peace, for a very short lease they held their land,
they quickly swerved from the flag they served — and they ran.

They lie down in the house of a hostile host
and can't tell the cure of the wound from its source:
when the smoke broke on them the news of the truce
they packed up, and scattered like starlings confused.

A gang of these from the battlefield shamefully skipped
to run crosscountry with cattle to the hills —
but when the farmer's harvest is all blown away
who cares who worked or idled on the harvest day?

These men I talk of, who walked no crooked ways,
their dried corn from kilns and tillage they freely gave —
their giving did not gain them the price of an egg —
they were simply plundered and cut to bits instead.

Since those dregs of plebs became most arrogant,
no bower or cowyard is safe from their camps —
it's a pity none has punished these cowherds' crimes
before they scattered so many to live in the wilds.

Though old women put rough linen from their heads
beneath a bishop's feet or on an abbot's bed,
if they're not abused by British troops and made game
they'll still be shamed by the neighbourly Mick McQuaid.

They eject all respect for the priest from our soil
though his dignified head was anointed with oil —
if he keeps the whore and the lecher apart
his head is smashed flat by a soldierly staff.

Like outlaws they hough and maul cattle on the land,
these rough root-eaters, these rabid reaper-bands:
whatever else the reason, justice must be blamed —
but I shall come back to their character again.

When army-less the English king fled from the field,
from the rage of retainers poor in loyalty,
the wall that held back horror in a hell
was ruptured by the surge of a violent swell.

Through the universe moved the angels from the depths
urging proud men to avoid what was good for them —
such propagation made my misery more acute
as their wiles so easily beguiled that very group.

The king, though ill-equiped, having little stock
and though his supporters were not much better off
in his deep fidelity to the men of this land
he sensed their distress far off in distant France.

The king decided in his mind to snatch them all
from the rage of the rain that threatened their downfall,
sent equipment and money, armoury and men,
and speeding over sea-crests, he came to guide them.

Though the surge of the flood broke the banks in its course
and Ireland's pulse convulsed in deliverance's throes,
the pilot did not contemplate delaying for one day
until his ship and cargo were docked at the quay.

The kind-hearted king who always hated wrong
his moderate orders in the market-place hung
condemning dissipation and the vagabond's rule
who were wild to undermine justice at the root.

In the proclamation's details they saw nothing wrong
but no heed paid to the name it issued from:
though gentle his advice to the uncivilised was
they didn't stop looting for one hour of the clock.

By ignoring the bestowing of this new-made *largesse*
which the Father poured down on his children's heads,
by the boiling of their violence beyond their duty's bounds
they looked for his reproach — and his reproach they found.

Unknown in the stories of skilled historians
is the whelping of such pups in any known land:
the arrogant and their plans have caused the disgrace
of gallows like shop-signs up in every place.

This gang (who gave scandal the like I never heard of
to the form of his laws, and his proclamations mocked)
are amazed they'll gain no titles as recompense
from the prudent king from whom poured down all that is.

This gang who never spared neither veil nor knapsack
and gambled away their fame in a mistaken clash —
how they expected mercy wise men cannot grasp
from the wealth-Giver who forgives the worst lapse.

In return for being plundered by servant-boy and bum
they stole the clothes and cows, the corn of the pitiful:
they preferred a band of hags to their wives at home —
it's queer that their careers have not been carved on stone.

To recite the crimes of these robbers and these thieves
would make this a prolix poem that would never cease —
as they cursed and swore by the ghosts of port and hill,
they did exactly what you'd expect of them.

All of our nobles by soldiers cut to bits,
all that were sent of our men to sea in cold ships,
all the exposure borne by the priests of our church —
it was that gang's anarchy which was the source of such.

Though I have tried, at last, haphazardly to tell
the cause of the loss of the discarded Articles,
look how late I've hesitated and no word wrote —
I, who have seen all round me gallows without rope.

The emptiness of every green territory states
that these fruitless gallows allude to their fate
and that the king is no longer held in awe:
let him take heed who sometimes needs to evade the law.

There was no win or loss that shadowed our people here
that for forty or more Novembers I did not weave:
it's time for me to throw away these futile poems —
they never brought corn or cattle to my door.

If my friends and relations say that I speak false
my overworked old bones will witness my reward:
their degraded station has half-blinded me —
I wouldn't cry my eyes out if this were flattery.

While success went to their heads when they had victory
and my spirit shivered when no news came to me —
I made no gains from writing from their spoils and graft,
no suit, no clothes, no horses, no safe-conduct pass.

I beg the Tradesman who made both cuckoo and fly
and the Hero who freed me from eternal fire,
and the Holy Ghost who cold hearts warms from ice,
that Irish men deserve a milder verse than mine.

If they became free I'd hoped to be quite well off
(minor civil servant, lackey to some toff):
but after all that, here in old shoes I stand —
so much for my writing for the men of Ireland.

'Strange is this noise . . .'

Strange is this noise that comes like a roar
from wretches who live and die unknown,
against one born of a noble clan
and trained in the ways of an intricate art.

I can see the plight of that unkempt gang —
not a jot of wit in their frothy harangue:
no poet should give them a second look —
they should cop themselves on and go back to their books.

It's strange they didn't conceal what they wrote
and they gave us their names as a matter of course:
like the pig with the bristles no man ever saw
they grunt at each syllable said by them all.

I cannot conceive that an Irish knight
or a fragile girl of a famous tribe
or a poet who follows the paths of the wise
could ever persecute good Maurice White.

His achievements deserve their love not hate
but spite finds it sweet a gift to berate.
Since he was anointed he guards his fame
and he has affection for his native place.

When we were beaten in the recent game
he got a knighthood from the head of state
and the scars on his side clearly explain
that against swords in battle he was not afraid.

He has faultless skill when he plays the harp
in a way unknown to that brainless gang:
he matches the lyrics with musical care
and his diction is beyond compare.

These midges harass him and hate him to sing
and his way with the gifts of the King of all skills:
if they try to defend their noisy reports
their trash will be stuffed back down their throats.

No well-woven cloth of grace or of wit
comes from these stupid insensible thicks
but a putrid flax is extracted unspun
which wounds all men like briers in mud.

If any gentleman had a hand
in weaving this offensive trash —
I don't like cursing, but my vision says
he'd be better off dead than made to pay.

Famous man, for whom I made this trivial music,
please accept it in all its crudeness:
it comes from your friend, restless and brooding,
your poor defender, Dáibhí O Bruadair.

'For a month . . .'

For a month I have been undergoing a siege,
  my brain and my body are worn —
I passed my early days in very foolish ways
  and I still have a long way to go.

To add to my griefs my endless bad deeds
  like worms torment me inside,
and now I can see I can do nothing here
  to further my children's pride.

I must briefly report what I said once before —
  though nobody listens to me —
that heavy's my grief since my wealth disappeared
  and debts mount up every year.

Now when gentlemen come to visit my home
  I can offer them no entertainment —
oh heavy's the yoke on a decent man broke,
  my poor heart inside me pains me.

Between such a crowd, in deluge and drouth,
  it's not easy to sleep without crying
and so many snares for the weak always wait,
  tormenting them wrongly or rightly.

I'm completely without either money or cows
  to repay these kind companions:
I pray to the King who made everything
  all of my debts to cancel.

It's better, I say, to be dead in your grave
    than trapped in the nets of misfortune
set by the gang who don't give a hang
    for the chain round my neck as a torture.

But the rest of the chiefs, so kind and genteel,
    with minds of no foreign designing —
I place all their lands into the hands
    of Him who bled on the cross and who died there.

Preserve them intact, their religion and rank,
    their children and wealth, without grieving:
set their places aside in the mansions of light,
    happy with You, I beseech You.

'The chaos that I see . . .'

The chaos that I see interrupts my sleep —
no love in laymen, no choirs in church I hear,
under cruel tortures naked humans writhe
while upstarts have their pride — at what a price!

Nowhere is honoured the arts of learned men,
no poets meet in contest with classic verse:
no one's poem now is worth a candle-snuff
unless he boasts a trunk half-full of stuff.

Even if 'tis full, no prince will back him up —
they can stand losing his support and love:
and though the mob have praised him in the past,
when he smiles at them now, they all but fart.

Every high son, puffed up with pomp and pride
who loves only cattle and lambs that are white,
though he would never give *me* a glance
in the street to salute him, *I* must doff my hat.

Druidical Athens, inventor of Art
cannot compare with these show-off upstarts:
no great man could match these blow-ins for state
while the poor lack the cash for food on their plates.

In a foundry if a fit it should seize
a fool of this gang who owns cows and bees,
on leaden tablets pens will engrave
the fact that he pissed in a holy place.

This litter's common trades — I don't mind them,
but the growing coldness of the nobles of Ireland:
that flock who used sweep gloom away from me
their love moves counter now to civility.

A plague on your ears and your crooked white head,
you have left me here to cry like a wretch,
for your pitiful death tells me my force is run,
since I knock nothing out of cows now, speckled or dun.

'O pity the man . . .'

O pity the man who won't spend his days
securing his goods before going astray:
I have anguish at home when the dawn turns red
and no one believes I have sense in my head.

Happy I lived in this fortress so bright,
in a true Irish fashion without any strife:
I followed whatever pursuit seemed to please
and well-minted money I scattered and spreed.

As long as a penny was bright in my hand
I seemed a clever and loveable man:
I had English wit and Latin pat
and my penmanship outdid the clerks'.

I got a salute from each husband and wife,
from each mother and son at breakfast inside:
if I asked for the town and half its contents
no one among them would refuse their consent.

I'd walk in and out and no one complained,
turn up at a house by night or by day —
and fine was their love as each said to me
'I pray you, sir, please, have a taste of this meal'.

But now my complexion is changed in their sight
and in my verse they can see nothing right:
since my milk turned sour in the eyes of the good
I've lost all respect, I'm a rider on foot.

It's proved I never abandoned my task
and the deformed I never attacked:
if I snapped without cause and I was unfair
the reaction to that would dirty my name.

Though up at the counter near fainting I stand
from morning till evening, my mouth would be parched:
if I offered security signed up and sealed
they won't even give me a half-pint of beer.

It's a thirsty old task, this ploughing alone
using an implement I'd never known:
my joints are swelled up from breaking this ground
and my fingers are numb from the shaft of this plough.

Let not my complaints mislead anyone
and let no one pass judgement on me too soon:
misfortune can only take half of the blame
for I was tricked in this crooked chess-game.

Miraculous Father, creator of all —
heaven and earth, planets and stars,
springtime and croptime, ice-time and warmth —
spare me from rage and answer my call.

A Whimsical Jingle

In August often the rich examine
the shining fancies in their caskets,
and what the earth brings forth in fragrance
lost blondes in London maidenheads.

Fullers froth at the mouth and shiver,
tanners go daft when deeply drinking:
surly girls are beaten under blankets
for refusing to give civil answers.

Screwpins are found in toolkits of blacksmiths
and hoops are tightly belted round barrels:
trumpets are often blown by boasters
and morons here are often blow-holes.

Wily hounds will often start off, sprinting,
sailors when cruising are often mad for liquor:
culchies with their cattle are contented
and sometimes boars run mad to Leinster.

Hobos lurk in woods to nail you
and upright men are often jailbirds:
chisels through timber are tapped by mallets
and, as for powder, all soldiers have it.

Poets are often buried in coffins
and a small man can wallop ruffians
and indeed (I can swear upon it)
the women of Munster don't piss in their bonnets.

Hooks are often baited for trout to nuzzle
and boozers lie plastered in pisspuddles:
a pair of mice you'll find in garrets
and the old are praised for their seeming smartness.

Curly hair in hoods and blinkers on cattle
and hussies have bustles like bales of cotton
and men are gloomy when they have no riches
and peace is better than contention.

Misers in dumps will harvest coltsfoot
at which even dogs turn up their noses:
corncrakes often crouch croaking in marshes
and old women often get cramps in their arses.

Pots are for boiling, pounds make up an income
and the heir has his white feet warm in slippers:
grass shrivels like seaweed when it's frosty
and servants often fart when they are caught short.

The forts of Dunkirk are completely without Paddies
and the craftsman's tool has no horns of badgers:
snobbish looks are always worn by lackeys —
in the presence of the pompous I feel backward.

Stops are found in print, curds and whey are mingled
and unwashed roots are snapped up by piglets:
if she's a hairy lady, I would still love her,
thin legs and all, above a girl with a muff on.

Now that there's no regard for sense in rhyme
and since it brings no joy to emulate the wise —
now that the men of Ireland can no longer rise —
a whimsical jingle is the verse that suits my mind.

Last Lines

Though made to suffer in this year abuse
and the bitterness this world has unloosed,
no careless language undermined my muse
but a lack of trash that would make my verse of use.

To form new friendships now, I have no strength
since those I loved to distant places went —
a shame my speeches to those exiled men
did not spur them to more perilous lengths.

9 *Martii* 1693/4